Wrestling
Greats

ANDRE
THE GIANT

Ross Davies

The Rosen Publishing Group, Inc.
New York

Published in 2001 by The Rosen Publishing Company, Inc.
29 East 21st Street, New York, NY 10010

Library of Congress Cataloging-in-Publication Data

Davies, Ross.
Andre the Giant / Ross Davies. — 1st ed.
p. cm. — (Wrestling greats)
Includes bibliographical references (p.) and index.
ISBN 0-8239-3430-6
1. Andre, the Giant, 1946–1993—Juvenile literature.
2. Wrestlers—France—Biography—Juvenile literature.
3. Motion picture actors and actresses—France—
Biography—Juvenile literature. [1. Andre, the Giant,
1946–1993. 2. Wrestlers.] I. Title.
GV1196.A53 D38 2001
796.812'092—dc21

00-013221

Manufactured in the United Stat

Contents

In a not-so-gentle moment, Andre the Giant finishes an opponent.

The Gentle Giant

"He was a hell of a guy and he always did his best. One thing I believe is that he was bigger than Gorgeous George, bigger than Hulk Hogan. He was the biggest box office attraction this sport has ever seen."

—Terry Funk, on Andre the Giant

For some people, the most memorable image of Andre the Giant is of that night in 1987, when he ripped a chain from Hulk Hogan's neck. Others may recall the nationally televised match in 1988 in which Andre finally won the world title from Hogan and gave the belt to Ted DiBiase. For others, their most vivid recollection of Andre may be of a seven-foot-four-inch man, hunched over in pain, unable to lift even the smallest wrestlers because of his back problems.

But these memories should not be Andre's legacy. Instead, fans should call to mind . . .

. . . *Andre, the gentle giant, happily shaking hands with a young, blond child who was no more than a third of his size. The child looked* up at Andre, not with fear, but with wonder and delight.

. . . the image of Andre enjoying a post-match dinner, living life to the fullest, because he knew he didn't have long to live.

. . . Andre—star of the movie The Princess Bride—A "wonderful, lovable, and a natural comedian," as one reviewer called him.

. . . the image of Andre, the king of nearly every ring he ever entered, vanquishing opponents with his enormous size and strength.

Andre the Giant with his costars Mandy Patinkin *(middle)* and Wallace Shawn *(bottom)* on the set of *The Princess Bride*

"I have had good fortune and I am grateful for my life," Andre told a *Sports Illustrated* interviewer. "If I were to die tomorrow, it would be with the knowledge that I have eaten more good food, drunk more beer and fine wine, had more friends, and seen more of the world than most men ever will. I have had everything in life but a family, and one day, I hope to have that. For now, I know a family wouldn't work because of all of the traveling I do, but who knows, one day, I might have a giant for a grandson."

Andre never did get married, but in a way, he did have a family—the fans who watched and adored him. "Andre truly was a gentle giant," wrote Bill

Apter in *Pro Wrestling Illustrated* magazine. "I covered dozens, if not hundreds, of his matches, and though he was vicious in the ring, he was incredibly kind to fans outside the ring. I can't imagine we'll ever again see anyone quite like him."

Andre was an amazing man. He was truly a giant. He was billed as standing seven feet four inches tall and weighing 520 pounds. He had gigantic hands and an overgrown face, and his upper body was the size of three men. Even outside the ring, he did things that defied the laws of believability.

One time in 1976, in Providence, Rhode Island, Andre and another wrestler went to a restaurant that offered an all-you-can-eat lobster special. The restaurant owners had no idea what they had gotten themselves into when Andre walked through the door. Andre and his friend ate twenty-eight lobsters, though Andre ate most of them. Restaurant patrons called their friends.

"Come down here!" they'd tell them. "You won't believe it until you see it!"

Andre wasn't trying to be mean or greedy by eating so many lobsters. He wasn't trying to run the restaurant owner out of business. He was simply hungry.

Andre was also a generous man. When he invited somebody out to dinner, he paid the bill. When somebody

Even Arnold Schwarzenegger couldn't beat Andre—at least not when it came to paying for dinner!

invited Andre out to dinner, he usually ended up paying the bill, too. One time, Andre was in Mexico shooting a movie with actor/strongman Arnold Schwarzenegger. Andre had taken Schwarzenegger out to dinner several times and had always picked up the check. After receiving several free meals, Schwarzenegger snuck over to the maitre d' and handed him his credit card. Suddenly, Schwarzenegger felt himself being picked up into the air. "When he had me up in the air, he turned me so I was facing him, and he said, 'I pay,'" Schwarzenegger later recalled to *New York* magazine.

Another time in Mexico, Andre invited Schwarzenegger to watch him wrestle.

After Andre won the match, he called for Schwarzenegger to join him in the ring.

"Take off your shirt," Andre told him. "They're all crazy for you to take off your shirt. I know that's what they're saying, I speak Spanish."

Schwarzenegger took off his shirt and posed for the crowd. When he was done, Schwarzenegger returned to his seat. Andre walked back to the dressing room, where he had himself a good laugh. He had played a practical joke on his friend—the fans hadn't been screaming for Schwarzenegger at all!

"Andre truly was a gentle giant."

-Bill Apter, *Pro Wrestling Illustrated*

"Nobody [cared] if I took my shirt off or not, but I fell for it," Schwarzenegger said. "Andre could do that to you."

Although at times he tried to play the part of the bad guy in the ring, anybody who really knew him didn't believe the act at all. The part he played in *The Princess Bride*—the warm-hearted gentle giant—was the real Andre.

"I was acting in the movie," Andre insisted. And he had to keep on insisting that he wasn't gentle, since at the time he was the most hated rulebreaker in the World Wrestling Federation (WWF).

2 A Big Boy with Big Dreams

Pretend that somebody with the power to grant your wishes made you the following offer: You will be one of the biggest men in the world. You will be a superstar at your chosen sport. People will love you. You will become famous and rich beyond your wildest imagination. You will appear in movies. You will meet famous people. Your face will appear on the covers of magazines everywhere, and everyone will know your name.

Your response would probably be "That sounds great. Now what's the catch?"

The catch is that you would have to cope with a rare disease that affects your glands—a disease that would have been with you since the day you were born. And during the last five or ten years of your life, your body would start to wear down. Eventually, the pain of lifting a child would be unbearable. And death would likely come to you before the age of fifty.

It's unlikely that anyone would accept such a deal. However, Andre the Giant never had a choice. He was born with this fate.

Andre the Giant was born Andre Rene Rousimoff on May 19, 1946, in Grenoble, France. Grenoble is a medium-sized city in southeast France, near the Italian border. There was nothing unusual about Andre's immediate family. He had two brothers and two sisters, all of normal height. His father, Stoeff, was six feet two inches. His mother, Marian, was five feet two inches.

When Stoeff Rousimoff saw his son's giant hands, he realized immediately that there was something unusual about his baby boy.

"Perhaps he will be a man to match my father," Stoeff Rousimoff said.

"But your father was a giant!" said Andre's mother. Andre's grandfather—who died before Andre was born—was seven feet eight inches and weighed more than 500 pounds.

Dad:

"I am the son of a giant. Why not be the father of one as well?" Andre's father replied.

Shortly after the birth of their son, Andre's parents found out that Andre had been born with acromegaly, a rare glandular disease that causes the body to manufacture too much growth hormone. As a result, the victim's head, face, hands, feet, and chest continue growing until they're oversized, though the arms and legs don't grow at the same rate. Eventually, Andre would have the hands, feet, and chest of a giant, but

**Andre had more trouble finding a
hotel bed that fit his large frame than
he had disposing of his opponents.**

the arms, legs, and trunk of a five-foot-six-inch man.

Giantism, as acromegaly is also called, is an abnormality. Few people who have it live past age fifty. The problem is that even when a person reaches the age when he or she is no longer growing, the body keeps on secreting growth hormones. As a result, the body keeps expanding, and the person ages more quickly.

Die before 50

As a young boy, Andre's dreams were as big as his body. By the time he was twelve, he was six feet three inches tall. His size, strength, and power enabled him to dominate in games against other kids. In fact, Andre was already bigger than most grown men.

One day, while young Andre and his father were raking hay on the farm, a man drove past the field in a Rolls Royce.

"Someday, I'll own a car like that," Andre said as he watched the Rolls disappear over the horizon.

"Stop dreaming and start raking," his father replied. "You may be a big boy, but that dream is too big even for you."

Andre refused to believe that any dream was too big for him. After all, when it came to rugby, soccer, and boxing, he was better than any other kid his age. He was even better than kids who were much older than he was.

Later that year, Andre left home and moved to Paris, where he got a job at a furniture-moving company. Later on, in 1963, when Andre was seventeen, he was working out in a gym when several professional wrestlers showed up. The wrestlers were amazed by his size. After talking with Andre and demonstrating some of their moves, they invited him to dinner. That night, over dinner, they told Andre what it was like to be a pro wrestler. Andre was intrigued by their stories. Perhaps this would be the path that would lead him to his dreams.

By the time he was twelve, Andre was 6'3" tall.

Andre got his big break in 1964, shortly after his eighteenth birthday. A wrestler had been injured and Andre stepped in to replace him. The crowd was amazed when they saw Andre, who by this time was six feet seven inches and weighed 245 pounds. Andre "the Butcher" Rousimoff won his first match easily.

Andre kept wrestling in France and kept winning matches. However, wrestling wasn't very popular in France, and Andre realized that he would have to move on if he wanted to become successful. After two years of wrestling and winning matches all over France, Andre got another big break.

In 1966, wrestler Frank Valois was passing through France on a wrestling tour that would also take him to England

and Germany. Valois was amazed the first time he saw Andre wrestle.

"What a thing to see he was!" Valois recalled. "Like a young mastiff." (A mastiff is a large, powerful guard dog.)

Valois had no trouble talking Andre into joining him for the rest of the tour in England and Germany. As Valois recalled, Andre had the time of his life.

"He loved to joke around," Valois said. "He was so happy in the game. In that first year or so he was around seven feet tall and he weighed 325 to 350 pounds, but he looked skinny because of his frame. I'm telling you, he broke up some rings and ring ropes learning to do the drop kicks and use the ropes right."

For several years, Andre and Valois wrestled all over Europe. Valois became Andre's business manager and best friend. He watched as a young, clumsy man developed into a strong, confident powerhouse. Andre continued to grow.

"One day, in Paris, Andre discovered that he could move a small car by himself," Valois recalled. "Andre would amuse himself by moving his friends' parked cars while they were around the corner at a restaurant or bar. He would pick up their cars and put them back down in small spaces between lamp posts, or he would turn them around to face the other way."

Despite these feats of strength, the legend of Andre "the Butcher" Rousimoff

This is Andre in 1982, when he was billed as Jean Ferré, "The Eighth Wonder of the World."

didn't travel outside of Europe. In those days, very few fans in the United States and Canada paid attention to wrestling in Europe. Even today, wrestling is a minor sport in Europe, compared to the United States, Canada, and Japan. At the time— the mid-1960s—most wrestling fans and promoters in North America weren't even aware that Andre existed.

Unknown outside of Europe

Andre was growing quickly. The unusual disease he had been born with had caused Andre to have two abnormal physical features: unusually heavy bone structure and relatively short legs. Andre's wrists would grow to twelve inches in circumference, more than five inches larger than those of an average person. His hands were massively long and wide. His fingers would grow to be so large that a silver dollar could pass through his rings. His head was oversized.

Meanwhile, Andre knew that if he wanted to move up in the world, he would have to leave Europe.

3 The Eighth Wonder of the World

For a boy who was born on a small farm in Grenoble, traveling to new places was a real thrill. By the age of twenty-two, Andre had wrestled in Algeria, South Africa, Morocco, Tunisia, England, and Scotland—and that's not even the whole list! In 1969, he toured New Zealand as "Monster Eiffel Tower." Sure, it was a funny name, but Monster Eiffel Tower was a big attraction.

Late in 1969, Isao Yoshihara, the president of a wrestling federation in Japan, traveled to Europe to look for new talent for his annual Grand Prix tournament. While in England, Yoshihara came across a sports writer who told him, "You should watch a man named Rousimoff. He's the biggest man I've ever seen, and he can wrestle, too."

The second Yoshihara saw Andre wrestle, he knew that he was looking at a big star. After Andre won his match that night, Yoshihara went to talk to the giant.

"I'd like you to wrestle in my Grand Prix tournament in Japan," Yoshihara said with the aid of an interpreter.

Andre was thrilled. He had never been to Japan, but he knew it was a hotbed for wrestling. If he was successful in Japan, there was a good chance the promoters in the United States would find out about him, too.

On January 3, 1970, Andre wrestled and won his first match in Japan. He stayed in Japan for six weeks, wrestling almost every night. In early February, with Andre's tour winding down, Verne Gagne arrived to defend his American Wrestling Association world heavyweight championship.

When Gagne saw Andre, his first thought was that Andre could be a great boxer. But Andre hadn't boxed since he was a child, and though he was flattered by Gagne's interest, he turned him down. After all, he really had no interest in doing anything but wrestling. At any rate, he was a hit in Japan. On January 18, 1970, Andre and Michael Nador beat Thunder Sugiyama and the Great Kusatsu in the International Wrestling Association world tag-team championship. They only held the belts for less than two weeks, but Andre loved the feeling of being a wrestling champion.

first belt

Andre's meeting with Verne Gagne was very fortuitous. Gagne, who owned the American Wrestling Association (AWA), was the first North American to become aware of Andre Rousimoff. Back home, Gagne told his friends about this amazing giant. Later that year, Andre left Europe and moved to Montréal, Canada, where he was an instant hit. Billed as Jean Ferré, "The Eighth Wonder of the World," Andre teamed with Edouard Carpentier in his first match in Montréal against Gary Brown and Fernand Ferchette. Carpentier and Andre won the first fall so easily that Andre agreed to wrestle the second fall by himself. He won that one, too.

"That man shouldn't be allowed into a ring," Brown complained. "He's the closest thing to Superman I've ever seen. I don't mind if a guy is seven feet tall or if he weighs 500 pounds, but I've never seen anybody that big and that strong move that fast!"

A few weeks later, Andre and Carpentier went up against Mad Dog

Vachon and Butcher Vachon. The Vachons were the most hated and most violent wrestlers in Canada. This would be Andre's first major test since coming to North America.

"He's the closest thing to Superman I've ever seen."

-Gary Brown on Andre the Giant

The Vachons used every trick in the book. They clawed, kicked, double-teamed, bit, and stomped Carpentier and Andre. Though Andre was bleeding badly, in an act of desperation, he whipped Butcher into the ropes and met him on the rebound with a forearm smash. Butcher suffered a concussion.

Then Andre bodyslammed Mad Dog five times in a row.

"It was like falling off a six-story building," said Mad Dog. Shortly after that match, the Vachons left Montréal for Chicago. Andre had not only proven himself against the best, but he had run "the best" out of town.

Andre kept piling up victories. He destroyed Abdullah the Butcher, a huge madman who liked to bite and injure his opponents. He humiliated Joe Leduc. He threw 450-pound Mountain Man around the ring like a ragdoll. The French-Canadians loved Andre because he spoke fluent French. The fans loved him for his friendly demeanor and wrestling skills.

"Andre was really living fast," Carpentier said. "As soon as he started making money, he bought a big white Cadillac and drove it all over town. He'd have a stogie in his mouth and had women draped all over him. I used to worry about him living so fast, but I guess he felt that he didn't have a long time to live, so he had to make the most of it."

Andre was beginning to get his first taste of stardom.

4 The Birth of Andre the Giant

Being seven feet five inches tall is not all it's cracked up to be. Finding hotel beds that fit is nearly impossible. Seats on buses, trains, and planes are always way too small. Dining out gets expensive—meals that would satisfy a normal-sized person are merely appetizers for the giants of the world.

In Québec, Andre "Jean Ferré" Rousimoff discovered yet another disadvantage to being big—he never lost a match. This may sound like a good thing, but it really isn't. There are only so many times fans will pay to watch a man easily win one wrestling match after another. The truth of the matter was that his dominance was becoming a bore.

Andre, as Jean Ferré, was winning his singles and tag-team matches so easily that promoters in Montréal started placing him in handicap matches against two or three opponents. He won most of those, too, often pinning two opponents at the same time. Even the best wrestlers fell prey to Andre in singles matches.

In 1971, Andre wrestled Don Leo Jonathan at the Montréal Forum. The Match of the Century, as newspaper writers called it, was also the battle of the giants— Jonathan was six feet nine inches tall and weighed 320 pounds. A crowd of over 20,000 jammed into the Forum. They were about to see something amazing. Andre, the mild-mannered giant, lost his temper and was disqualified for picking up Jonathan and tossing him out of the ring. Andre's message was clear: "I'm the nicest guy in the world, but if you get me mad, watch out!"

News about Andre soon spread to the United States, where promoters were eager to book him into matches in their cities. Andre started wrestling in Verne Gagne's AWA (still as Jean Ferré), where he had some great matches against

"Superstar" Billy Graham, one of the best wrestlers of the era. Graham shocked everyone one night when he caught Andre off balance and slammed him to the mat. It was the first time Andre had ever been bodyslammed.

"At the time, nobody took him off his feet," Graham said.

In 1971, Andre was named Rookie of the Year by *Wrestling Yearbook* magazine. He was considered to be the greatest French wrestler since Edouard Carpentier. Nobody—except for one man—doubted that Andre was even a better wrestler than Carpentier. That one man was Mad Dog Vachon. Vachon, who had returned from the United States, sought revenge against Andre for the defeat in the tag-team match a year and a half earlier. In 1972, Mad Dog challenged Andre to a match in Verdun, in his home province of Québec. It was going to be a tough match. Mad Dog had the home advantage. But Andre welcomed the challenge.

"I've been going along right on schedule," Andre said. "I began by wrestling preliminary opponents and increased my level of competition as I improved. I worked at it like a boxer does, getting a certain number of matches under my belt before tangling with the real big ones. I never felt I was ready to go in against Mad Dog one-on-one before. I'd wrestled him and his brother in a tag-team match, but Ed Carpentier had been my partner. It's one thing to have Edouard to fall back on if you're in trouble, but going alone against Mad Dog, I knew there'd be no Carpentier to help me out. The thing is, though, sooner or later you've got to prove to yourself whether you're just another wrestler or something special. And around here the only way you find out is by facing Mad Dog Vachon."

The small arena in Verdun was packed for the match. Andre was nervous and Vachon was confident, as always. Mad Dog attacked early and tried to gouge out Andre's eyes. Each time they got close, Vachon would go for the eyes. Carpentier, who was sitting at ringside, watched nervously as Andre stumbled blindly around the

Andre's 1972 one-on-one matchup against Mad Dog Vachon in Québec was ruled a no contest because Vachon blinded the referee.

ring. Then Vachon started biting Andre. But Vachon got too close. Andre grabbed him, lifted him high for a minute, and then smashed him to the canvas. Andre threw Vachon all over the place while simultaneously protecting his eyes from Vachon's clawing hands.

Vachon panicked and started swinging his fists, and Andre let go with a left hook that almost knocked Vachon out. Then Vachon attacked the referee and went after his eyes. Vachon then turned his attention to Andre and gouged his eyes. Unable to watch anymore, Carpentier stormed into the ring to replace the blinded referee. Vachon—who hated Carpentier, attacked both him and Andre.

The timekeeper rang the bell and the match was ruled a no contest.

"I'd have beaten him had he not blinded the referee," Andre insisted.

The Québec fans agreed with Andre that nobody who wrestled fair and square stood a chance against him. Because of this, little by little, attendance at Andre's matches dwindled. The fans simply became bored. Andre was bored, too. He was ready for a new challenge. Once again, Valois came to his rescue. He arranged for Andre to meet with World Wide Wrestling Federation promoter Vince McMahon Sr. in New York.

McMahon would never forget the first time he saw Andre. "My initial

Andre's career took off when Vince McMahon Sr., who nicknamed him "the Giant," began promoting him.

reaction was, 'My God, I never saw such a man,'" McMahon recalled. "I'd seen photographs and videotapes, of course, and I knew Andre was seven feet four inches and over 400 pounds, but I simply wasn't prepared for how he looked up close. He was unlike anything I'd ever seen before, and I knew he could become the number one draw in wrestling."

McMahon concluded that Andre had wrestled too many times in Québec. McMahon was a master crowd manipulator. Throughout the 1960s and 1970s, the WWWF world heavyweight title was rarely defended on television. McMahon figured that if the fans got world title matches for free on television, they wouldn't pay for tickets to see them at arenas. A person could count on one hand the number of times Bruno Sammartino defended the WWWF world title on TV during his twelve years as champion.

"I saw right away that Andre needed to be booked into a place no more than a few times a year," McMahon said. "Most of our men work one of our circuits for a while and then move to another. It keeps things fresh. For instance, a guy may work New England for a few months and then go to the South and then on out to spend some time with Verne Gagne in Minneapolis. But Andre's different. The whole world is his circuit."

McMahon was very shrewd. He decided to change Andre's name from Jean Ferré to Andre the Giant. In 1973, Andre the Giant wrestled his first WWWF match at Madison Square Garden. The fans in New York City were amazed by his size and strength. Then McMahon sent Andre to Japan, Australia, and all over Europe. Andre would stay a week or two in an area, win his matches, and then move on to another area. At first, people wanted to see him as a novelty, but then they wanted to see more and more of him. They realized that he wasn't just a peculiarity. He was an amazing athlete.

"After seeing him, they recognized he wasn't a one-night stand," Valois said.

The fans couldn't get enough of Andre and neither could the promoters. In 1973 and 1974, Andre broke attendance records all over the United States. He wrestled in handicap matches and battle royals and won them all. In 1974, Andre made over $400,000. *The Guinness Book of World Records* listed him as the highest paid wrestler ever.

The Wrestler Versus the Boxer

As Andre's fame grew, there were times when he fondly remembered that long-ago conversation with his father in the hayfield. "Stop dreaming and start raking," his father had said when Andre mused that he would one day own a Rolls Royce. "You may be a big boy, but that dream is too big even for you."

Suddenly, no dream was too big for Andre. He had the world at his feet. He was

By 1976, when he appeared on The Mike Douglas Show with Verne Gagne, Chris Taylor, and Jerry Lewis, Andre the Giant had become a household name.

one of the only wrestlers who had become a household name even in homes where people weren't wrestling fans. Andre appeared on *The Tonight Show*, the popular late-night talk show, and *The Mike Douglas Show* along with comedian Jerry Lewis. He even did guest appearances on the action TV show *The Six Million Dollar Man*—starring Lee Majors as the bionic man—where he played a character called Bigfoot.

"It was a lot of fun doing the show," Andre said. "I did my own stunts. After all, how were they going to find a stand-in who is seven foot five and weighs over 400 pounds? It got a little rough for me at times. There was the one scene where Steve Austin (actor Lee Majors) gets the upper hand and sends me rolling down this huge wooded hill. I rolled and rolled until I finally came to the bottom and almost crashed into the lighting equipment on the set. Because of some technical problems, we had to do that scene five times. By the third time, I was ready to murder the guy who kept yelling, 'We'll have to do that scene again!'"

Throughout Andre's career, wrestling promoters had always fantasized about his marketing potential. Verne Gagne had thought about turning him into a boxer, and Vince McMahon saw dollar signs whenever Andre walked into a room. In July 1975, the Washington Redskins of the National Football League realized that Andre belonged on a football field.

Tim Temerario, the Redskins' personnel director, told the story of how Washington coach George Allen became interested in Andre.

"After the draft, George Allen said he would like to sign someone unusual, maybe about seven feet tall," Temerario told a press conference. "I had heard about this wrestler and traced him through Vince McMahon. When he told me how much Andre earned, I was a little bit put off. It would take a long time to get him ready, but I knew he was quick and had the agility to be a defensive tackle or end. We were interested, and I talked to Allen about it."

The problem was, Andre was making $400,000 a year in the ring—more than even the best football players were earning. Andre was intrigued and flattered by the Redskins' offer, but he wasn't going to start playing football for less money than he was earning. The Redskins offered him a tryout, but Andre decided not to accept

Made too much

Andre turned it down

their offer (much to the relief of every other quarterback in the NFL).

In between all of these distractions, Andre found time to wrestle. He won numerous battle royals. He defeated Japanese star Kenta Kobayashi in Japan. In early 1976, he received his first match against National Wrestling Alliance (NWA) world champion Terry Funk, one of the toughest wrestlers in the world.

Andre was nervous before the match against Funk. He paced up and down in the locker room. When the match started, both men were wary of each other. Funk and Andre were careful not to make a mistake that would cost either one the match. After ten minutes, Andre and Funk finally tore into each other. The match ended when *1976* Andre hurled Funk over the rope. Funk was awarded the match by disqualification.

That year, Andre had one of his most famous matches ever—a wrestler vs. boxer match against heavyweight contender Chuck Wepner. The match was to be held on June 25, 1976, at Shea Stadium in Queens, New York. That same night, another boxer vs. wrestler match would be held in Tokyo, Japan between boxing heavyweight champion Muhammad Ali and Japanese wrestling champion Antonio Inoki.

"This will just be exercise," Andre promised when the bout was announced.

Wepner was concerned. "He's got a head as big as a watermelon held sideways and a fifty-six-inch waist," he said. "I told my manager to bring extra gloves. I may lose one in his belly."

Wepner was one of the few people in the world who thought that he had a chance against Andre.

"These wrestlers aren't used to constant pressure," Wepner said. "I must have had over 200 street fights and I don't remember losing any of them. I was the toughest kid in the neighborhood when I was fourteen."

The one thing that Wepner didn't realize was that Andre was one of the toughest people in the world when he was fourteen.

During the buildup to the matches, Ali stood beside Andre, comparing the size of

A comparison of each wrestler's measurements illustrates the huge advantage Andre had over his sizable opponent:

WEPNER		ANDRE
230	**Weight**	440
6'5"	**Height**	7'4"
72"	**Reach**	87"
46"	**Chest**	60"
17 1/2"	**Biceps**	20 1/2"
13 1/2"	**Forearm**	16"
36"	**Waist**	56"
27"	**Thigh**	31 1/2"
16"	**Calf**	19"
18"	**Neck**	23"
8 1/2"	**Wrist**	12 1/2"
13"	**Fist**	16"
9"	**Ankle**	16"

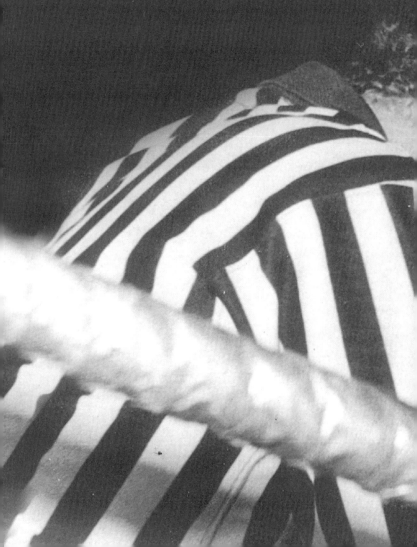

Heavyweight boxer Chuck Wepner was no match for Andre the Giant in the famous wrestler vs. boxer match at Shea Stadium in 1976.

Ali Posed w/ Andre

their hands. Ali had huge paws, but Andre's positively dwarfed his. Seeing this, Ali called Wepner on the phone and told him, "If he falls on you, you're through. He's a big man. He'll hit you so hard it will jar your kinfolk in Germany. You got a tough fight and a lot of guts to be fighting this guy." Ali was glad he was fighting Inoki, and not Andre.

Ali called Chuck

"It will be a new experience for me to fight a boxer," Andre said. "But I have confidence that I will beat Wepner and after I finish him, I'll take on Ali, if he can whip Inoki, which I doubt."

A crowd of over 35,000 fans attended the Andre vs. Wepner match, and nobody who saw the match will ever forget what they witnessed.

Wepner moved cautiously after the opening bell. For the first two rounds, he circled Andre and stayed at least an arm's length from his gigantic opponent. Despite his pre-match boasting, Wepner was clearly scared. Andre was patient.

In the third round, Wepner took a chance. He wound up and hit Andre with a solid right, but Andre acted as if he had *3rd round* only been stung by a mosquito. He picked up Wepner, lifted him in the air, and threw him over the top rope and into the first row of seats. Wepner called it quits. The match was over.

Wepner never asked for a rematch. And Ali, who battled to a draw with Inoki, stayed as far away from Andre as possible.

6 Andre Versus Hogan, Part I

In 1987, the most anticipated wrestling match ever—Andre the Giant vs. Hulk Hogan at WrestleMania III—took place at the Silverdome in Pontiac, Michigan. The biggest crowd ever assembled for a wrestling match turned out to witness Andre and Hogan battle in the main event. According to the WWF, this was the first time the former friends had ever wrestled each other.

However, the truth of the matter was *First time* that in 1978, Andre wrestled Hogan for the first time at the Houston Farm Center in *1978* Dothan, Alabama, where Andre won. By the time they met again in 1980, a lot had happened to both men. Andre had won the National Wrestling Alliance Australian tag-team title with Ron Miller and the NWA *Titles* United States tag-team title with Dusty Rhodes. He had triumphed over superstar tough guy Bruiser Brody in St. Louis, and he had also won the NWA Florida tag-team title with Dusty Rhodes.

Meanwhile, Hogan, who made his professional debut in 1978, had become *Hogan a bad guy* one of the most hated men in wrestling. At six feet eight inches, 275 pounds of pure

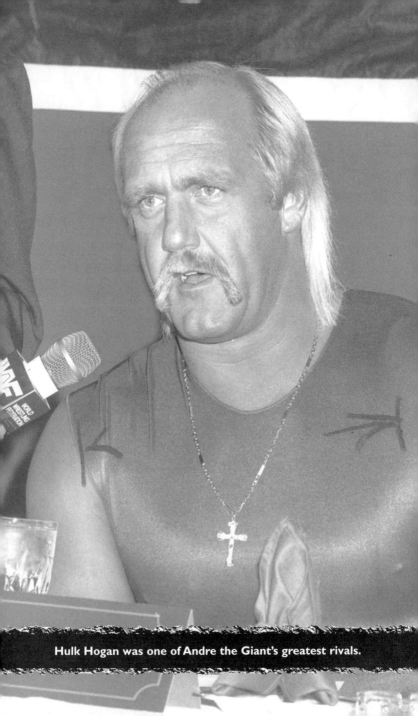

Hulk Hogan was one of Andre the Giant's greatest rivals.

muscle, Hogan was a mean guy who always wore a scowl and delighted in injuring his opponents. He was hungry for stardom and was managed by Freddie Blassie, a notorious manager of rulebreakers.

The Andre vs. Hogan feud started at a WWF television taping, when Hogan whipped Andre with a lariat. The attack left Andre lying on the mat with blood pouring out of his head. Hogan had no mercy. He picked up Andre and bodyslammed him to the ground.

Andre and Hogan feuded all over the United States, as well as in Canada and Japan. On August 2, 1980, Andre and Hogan battled to a draw at the Superdome Spectacular in New Orleans. Seven days later, a crowd of 35,771 jammed into Shea Stadium to watch Andre and Hogan go at it again. This time, Andre pinned Hogan. The match finished second in the balloting for *Pro Wrestling Illustrated*'s Match of the Year.

Hogan a cheater

Andre, who never cheated, never failed to be riled by Hogan's rule-breaking.

"I prefer to wrestle according to the rules, because I do not have to cheat to win a match," Andre said. "A small man does not have to cheat, either. I think the best wrestler or the strongest man should win, not the one who sticks his finger in your eye."

As much as Andre hated Hogan, there was one wrestler he detested even more—Killer Khan, a 280-pound villain who always seemed more interested in harming his opponents than beating them. On April 13, 1981, Andre and Khan met in Rochester, New York, for a match that would be named Match of the Year by *Pro Wrestling Illustrated.* *Match of the Year*

During the match, Khan was lying on the mat and Andre climbed to the top turnbuckle and leaped onto Khan. Andre landed badly. He could feel something happen to his left ankle. Though he knew something was wrong, he didn't realize that his ankle *Broken ankle* was broken. Andre finished the match and won, but the damage had been done.

The hospital that treated him had never dealt with a patient as big as Andre. The doctor used the largest screws available

surgery

For many years, wrestling fans couldn't get enough of the battle for supremacy between Andre the Giant and Hulk Hogan.

to fix Andre's ankle. They encased his ankle in a huge cast, but, the hospital's crutches weren't nearly long enough. The injury forced Andre to miss several matches and lose a lot of money.

"I hate Khan and Blassie," Andre said. "I have hated Hulk Hogan, Ernie Ladd, and others, but none as much as Khan. Well, Khan, he thinks he is a giant. But he is only six feet six inches, and I'm seven feet five inches, and I weigh close to 500 pounds. So Khan, I will destroy you!" Sure enough, Andre returned to the ring in late July and got his revenge against Khan and Blassie.

Over the next five years, Andre piled up victories against every opponent he faced. Ernie Ladd, Blackjack Mulligan, and

rematch

Andre Versus Hogan, Part I

Ken Patera fell by the wayside. At the WWF's WrestleMania I in 1985, Andre bodyslammed Big John Studd, who was over seven feet tall. At WrestleMania II in Chicago, Andre won a battle royal that included NFL lineman William "Refriger-ator" Perry and others.

*Wrestlmania #2
Battle Royal - fridge*

Andre became the first wrestler pro-filed by *Sports Illustrated* magazine. The article was reprinted in *Reader's Digest.* *SI.*

After twenty-two years in the sport, Andre was still one of the most successful and popular wrestlers in the world.

But when Andre looked back over his career, he realized that something was missing—he had never won the world heavyweight title.

7 Andre Versus Hogan, Part II

By 1987, only one man in wrestling was more popular than Andre. Ironically, that man was Hulk Hogan, who seven years earlier had been the bad guy in his feud with Andre.

Thanks to Hogan, wrestling had become more popular than ever. Hulkamania was all the rage. Fans all over the world were wearing the Hulkster's trademark red and yellow shirts and headbands.

Hogan had won the WWF world championship in 1984 and seemed as though he was invincible.

Despite their turbulent past, Andre and Hogan had become close friends. They were both fan favorites in the WWF, and as such were on the same side in battles against the federation's rulebreakers and bad guys. However, at the beginning of 1987, Andre started to have second thoughts about his so-called friend. "If Hogan's my friend," Andre wondered, "then how come he's never offered me a title shot?" Around the same time, manager Bobby Heenan began suggesting the same thing to Andre.

Both good guys

The more Andre thought about it, the angrier he became. Ultimately, Andre demanded a title match, but Hogan refused. Finally, in a dramatic confrontation seen by millions of television viewers, Andre ripped a chain from around Hogan's neck. Blood trickled down Hogan's chest and the feud was on.

With that simple action, Andre had gone from being one of the most beloved men in wrestling to being one of the most hated. *Andre became a hero*

Immediately, the WWF signed Andre and Hogan to meet at WrestleMania III on March 29, 1987. Promoters knew that a normal wrestling arena wouldn't be big enough for this event so the match was held at a football stadium—the Silverdome in Pontiac, Michigan. The show sold out two weeks in advance. The crowd of 93,173 broke every indoor wrestling attendance and gate record.

Andre vs. Hogan was the most anticipated match in wrestling history. As bell time approached, both men paced nervously in their locker rooms. After the ring announcer introduced Andre and Hogan, the stadium thundered with the sound of the crowd's applause. Finally, after nearly a month of anticipation, the timekeeper rang the bell to start the match.

Andre attacked early and slammed Hogan to the mat. With only fifty-four seconds gone in the match, Andre covered Hogan for the pin. The referee counted to two, and Hogan lifted his shoulder just before the three count. In the minds of many people, including Bobby Heenan, the slow count had robbed Andre of the world title.

Andre dominated the match. At one point, he wrapped his massive arms around Hogan's torso and held him in a bear hug for nearly three minutes. Somehow, Hogan broke the hold. Andre continued his assault by viciously slamming Hogan to the mat. Andre was wrestling like a hungry animal. Nobody could remember ever seeing him so angry.

But then, with over eleven minutes gone in the match, the impossible happened. Hogan whipped Andre off the ropes and kicked him in the chest. A stunned Andre could do nothing to resist Hogan's all-out assault. Andre was off balance and staggering. He had failed to put away the Hulkster when he had the chance. Now he was going to pay for his mistake. The crowd rose to its feet. Hogan wrapped his arms around Andre's body, lifted him with all his might, and slammed him to the mat!

Three seconds later, Hogan pinned Andre to retain the world title.

Andre was incensed. Afterward, he complained about the slow three count early in the match. He felt that he had pinned Hogan and that he deserved to be

Andre faces off against Hogan at a New York press conference before squaring off for "The Main Event" in 1988.

world champion. But Andre's complaints fell on deaf ears.

Wrestling fans clamored for a rematch, but Hogan was reluctant to give Andre another shot at the title. At the 1987 Survivor Series, Andre teamed with One Man Gang, King Kong Bundy, Butch Reed, and Rick Rude to beat Hogan, Bam Bam Bigelow, Paul Orndorff, Don Muraco, and Ken Patera in an elimination match. Andre pinned Bigelow to win the match for his team, but the man he really wanted was Hogan.

Rematch

On February 5, 1988, Andre had a rematch against Hogan in Indianapolis, Indiana. The rematch, billed as "The Main Event," was aired on TV on NBC. It

NBC

In 1988, wrestling fans began to notice Andre's increasing anger and ferocity in the ring.

marked wrestling's return to prime-time network television for the first time in more than thirty years.

However, by that time, Andre had sold his soul to the devil. The devil was Ted DiBiase, the so-called Million Dollar Man. Having failed to win the WWF world title fairly, DiBiase tried to do the next best thing (in his own crooked mind)—he offered to buy the belt from Andre.

A national television audience watched raptly as Hogan and Andre went at it for the second time. Andre, who was even angrier than he was in the first match, attacked Hogan at the contract signing a month earlier, and he continued his attack when the bell rang. Hogan had several chances to pin Andre, but couldn't finish the job. Late in the match, Andre bodyslammed Hogan and covered him for a pin attempt. Referee Dave Hebner made the count. The Hulkster clearly kicked out at the count of two, but Hebner made the three count anyway. As the crowd watched in shock, Hebner handed the belt to Andre.

Quick count

Evil Twin

Then the unthinkable happened, and Andre handed the belt to DiBiase. He had agreed to sell the belt to his manager. Nobody had ever done anything like this before!

The confusion, however, had only just begun. A second referee, who looked identical to the first, stumbled into the ring.

Both men looked exactly like Dave Hebner. A confused Hogan angrily grabbed both men by their shirts. He wanted to know exactly what was going on.

What had happened was one of the most spectacular schemes ever: DiBiase had paid off Earl Hebner, Dave's identical twin brother, to referee the match and cheat on Andre's behalf.

Evil Ref

<u>Before the match, Andre and DiBiase had tied up Dave in a back room.</u>

The incidents at The Main Event threw the wrestling world into upheaval. A few days later, WWF president Jack Tunney made this confusing ruling: Andre's pin of Hogan was valid, despite the impostor referee, but Andre had violated the rules by giving the belt to DiBiase. The transaction was ruled invalid. The title was declared vacant. Tunney ordered a tournament to be held at WrestleMania IV.

The events of The Main Event were not only tragic for wrestling, they were tragic for Andre, too. Although Andre was well past his prime and constantly suffering from serious pain because of giantism, he was capable of beating Hogan. He had proven that at WrestleMania III. He didn't need an impostor referee. And he certainly should have had more respect for the belt than to give it to DiBiase. Andre had worked all of his life for this opportunity, but when he got it, he had thrown it away.

On March 27, 1988, at WrestleMania IV, Andre and Hogan battled to a draw in the second round of the world title tournament. Because of the draw, both men were eliminated from the tournament. Randy Savage went on to win his first WWF world title.

In the back of his mind, Andre must have known that the title should have been his.

A Giant Legacy

8

With a new champion holding the WWF world heavyweight title, Andre turned his attention to Randy Savage. But despite his ferocity, Andre couldn't beat Savage for the belt. At SummerSlam '88, Hogan and Savage beat Andre and DiBiase, known as the Megabucks, in the main event. Andre feuded with fan favorites Hacksaw Duggan, Jake "the Snake" Roberts, and Bam Bam Bigelow.

Andre's ferocity was stunning. He seemingly loved to hurt his opponents. He would cackle with delight whenever he wrapped his huge hands around an opponent's throat. Whatever happened to the gentle giant? His bitterness was sad to witness. In 1988, Andre the Giant was voted Most Hated Wrestler of the Year by the readers of *Pro Wrestling Illustrated.*

Voted most
hated

"What has happened to Andre over the past two years is one of the saddest stories in wrestling history," a wrestling fan wrote to the magazine. "While he was never what you could call a great wrestler, I always had a lot of respect for Andre. Now he's a maniac. He doesn't even show any remorse."

For a while, Andre wore a mask and called himself the Giant Machine. Of course, a mask couldn't disguise Andre. His enormous size always gave him away.

Nonetheless, all was not completely lost for Andre. He was the first man inducted into the WWF Hall of Fame, and he starred in the popular movie *The Princess Bride* with Peter Falk and Billy Crystal. By that time, however, his body was breaking down.

During the filming of the movie, actress Robin Wright was supposed to jump out of a castle window and into Andre's arms. The shot was designed so that Wright would be lifted just above the camera and dropped gently only a

Andre couldn't hide the fact that he was in terrible pain at the end of his career.

foot or two into Andre's arms. On the first take, Andre gasped when he caught her, even though she couldn't have weighed more than 120 pounds. Then, Andre fell to his knees and almost turned white. He clutched his back in pain.

Andre had always known his life would be short. In his final years as a wrestler, he wore a back brace under his wrestling tights. By the late 1980s, Andre couldn't hide the fact that he was in tremendous pain. He could barely move in the ring. He visibly winced when he lifted opponents who, at one time, he would have easily thrown around the ring.

On December 13, 1989, Andre teamed with Haku to beat Demolition for his first WWF world tag-team title. Their reign didn't last long. At WrestleMania VI, Andre and Haku lost the belts to Demolition. Andre and manager Bobby Heenan broke up when Heenan blamed the loss on Andre.

Andre had one more go-round as a fan favorite after Earthquake attacked him in 1991. However, he was in too much pain, and the battle of big men never took place.

Andre made his final United States wrestling appearance at World Championship Wrestling's Clash of the Champions on September 2, 1992, in Atlanta. It was an emotional scene as Andre, who had recently undergone knee surgery, walked to the ring with the aid of two canes. The crowd gave

Andre's bullying attack on pint-sized referee Dick Kroll contributed to his being voted the most hated wrestler in 1988.

Andre a standing ovation. He didn't wrestle that night. He couldn't wrestle.

Andre wrestled the final match of his career on December 4, 1992, at Budokan Hall in Japan. He teamed with long-time rival Shohei Baba and Rusher Kimura to beat Haruka Eigen, Motoshi Okuma, and Masa Fuchi.

After his last match, Andre returned to his roots. He moved to a 200-acre estate in North Carolina, where he raised sheep and quarterhorses. Then, on January 9, 1993, Andre learned that his father was dying. Andre flew home to France. His father died on January 15.

On January 27, 1993, Andre's chauffeur came to pick him up from his hotel in France. Andre never answered the phone in his room. The hotel staff broke down the door and found him dead. He was forty-six years old.

"He was lying in his bed when they found him," recalled long-time friend Frenchie Bernard. "He just went to sleep and never woke up again."

Andre never had a chance to say goodbye to his friends and his millions of fans. He died quietly, gently, and probably painlessly.

"We do not live long, the big and the small," Andre had said to Billy Crystal during the filming of *The Princess Bride*. But it's doubtful that anybody has ever lived bigger than Andre the Giant.

Glossary

battle royal Free-for-all match in which twenty or more wrestlers compete in the ring at the same time. The object is to eliminate your opponents by tossing them over the top rope, and to be the last person remaining in the ring.

bell time Starting time for a wrestling card.

bodyslam Offensive move in which the attacker scoops up his or her opponent and slams him or her viciously to the mat.

defensive line In football, the defensive players on the line of scrimmage.

disqualification Ruling by the referee in which a wrestler automatically loses a match for violating a rule.

draw Outcome in a wrestling match in which a winner isn't declared, usually when the designated time limit is reached without either side winning.

first fall The first fall in a best two-of-three-falls match.

gate record Money collected for tickets sold.

handicap match Wrestling match in which one team has more wrestlers than the other team, or in which a single wrestler competes against two or more wrestlers.

kinfolk Relatives.

main event The featured match at a wrestling show, usually the last match of the night.

preliminary opponents The wrestlers who compete in the earliest matches on a wrestling card; generally, the ones with the worst records.

rulebreaker   In wrestling, a bad guy, generally someone disliked by the fans. So-called because he or she violates the rulebook.

stogie   Cigar.

turnbuckle   Padded area in all four corners where the ropes meet.

For More Information

Magazines

Inside Wrestling, Pro Wrestling Illustrated, Wrestle America, The Wrestler, and *Wrestling Superstars*
London Publishing Co.
7002 West Butler Pike
Ambler, PA 19002

WCW Magazine
P.O. Box 420235
Palm Coast, FL 32142-0235

WOW Magazine
McMillen Communications
P.O. Box 500
Missouri City, TX 77459-9904
e-mail: woworder@mcmillencomm.com
Web site: http://www.wowmagazine.com

Web Sites

Dory Funk's Web Site
http://www.dory-funk.com

Professional Wrestling Online Museum
http://www.wrestlingmuseum.com

Pro Wrestling Torch
http://www.pwtorch.com

World Championship Wrestling
http://www.wcw.com

World Wrestling Federation
http://www.wwf.com

For Further Reading

Albano, Lou, Bert Randolph Sugar, and
    Michael Benson. *The Complete
    Idiot's Guide to Pro Wrestling.* 2nd
    ed. New York: Alpha Books, 2000.

Archer, Jeff. *Theater in a Squared
    Circle.* New York: White-Boucke
    Publishing, 1998.

Cohen, Dan. *Wrestling Renegades: An
    In-Depth Look at Today's
    Superstars of Pro Wrestling.* New
    York: Archway, 1999.

Farley, Cal. *Two Thousand Sons: The Story of Cal Farley's Boys Ranch.* Blaine, WA: Phoenix Publishing, 1987.

Hofstede, David. *Slammin': Wrestling's Greatest Heroes and Villains.* New York: ECW Press, 1999.

Mazer, Sharon. *Professional Wrestling: Sport and Spectacle.* Jackson, MS: University Press of Mississippi, 1998.

Myers, Robert. *The Professional Wrestling Trivia Book.* Boston: Branden Books, 1999.

Works Cited

"Andre `The Giant' Rousimoff." *Wrestling Observer Newsletter,* February 8, 1993, pp. 1–6.

"Editors' Award: Andre the Giant." *Pro Wrestling Illustrated,* March 1994, p. 58.

Goldman, William. "Requiem for a Heavyweight." *New York,* February 15, 1993, p. 16

Guback, Steve. "Redskins May Be Ready to Land a Real Biggie." *The Washington Star,* July 9, 1975, p. C-5.

"Jean Ferre—Rookie of the Year."
Wrestling Yearbook, 1972, pp. 14-52.

"Match of the Year: Hulk Hogan vs. Andre
the Giant." *Pro Wrestling Illustrated,*
March 1989, p. 51.

Pepe, Phil. "Cocky Ali Warns Wepner: Don't
Be Andre's Fall Guy." *Daily News,*
June 23, 1976: p. 85.

Reed, Marshall. "Wepner Faces Giant
Problem." *Long Island Press,*
June 24, 1976.

Index

Photo Credits

All photos courtesy of *Pro Wrestling Illustrated* except p. 8 © Everett Collection; pp. 12, 80–81 © AP/Worldwide.

Series Design and Layout

Geri Giordano